My Will or Thine

My Will or Thine

answering difficult questions surrounding LDS priesthood blessings

B. RUSSELL McCONKIE

My Will or Thine: Answering Difficult Questions Surrounding LDS
Priesthood Blessings
by B. Russell McConkie
©2015 B. Russell McConkie

ISBN-13: 978-0989987356
ISBN-10: 0989987353

This book is based on actual events. Some of the names have been
changed to protect the privacy of individuals involved.

Content and copy editing: Jennifer Lovell, Mark Young
Beta readers and proofreaders: Melanie Elkins, Nancy Farnworth,
Luke Randall, Jill Randall, Betsy Polish, JoBeth Morrison, Bryan
Elkins, Kristynn Runyan, LaNetta Maxfield, Lorraine Robinson

Cover design by Russell Elkins
Cover photo by Jammie Elkins Photography
Interior ebook formatting and print book design: Russell Elkins
Published by Inky's Nest Publishing

1st edition
First printed in 2015 in the United States of America

table of contents

budding questions

$\mathbf{A}$ few years ago I found myself standing in the dark in the center of my brother's large walk-in closet. I was staring out the small window at the thin skiff of snow now covering the ground while holding my infant son close to my chest. It was Christmas Eve and I could hear the rest of my extended family downstairs laughing, playing games, and enjoying each other's company.

My little boy was finally asleep in my arms. This was his first time being sick with a fever, so he had been inconsolable and confused about how his body felt. For hours on end we had been going through the same routine. He was so uncomfortable that he would squirm and wiggle, trying to break away from me and his discomfort. I would then give in and place him on the floor where he would crawl away only to return seconds later when he realized he was unable to escape his misery and he hoped to find comfort in Daddy's arms again. Over and over we did this until he was so exhausted that sleep finally overtook him.

It was while I stood there, pressing my cheek to his warm forehead, that I began to think more deeply about questions I had been pondering for many years. I contemplated The Church of Jesus Christ of Latter-day Saints' (LDS) teachings concerning priesthood blessings of healing and comfort.

Although my baby boy was hurting and had a pretty high fever, I felt confident his illness was not serious and would soon pass. But as I stood there holding him in the dark, I pondered the importance of priesthood blessings in more serious circumstances. What if my son were to ever be in a dire situation? As a Melchizedek priesthood holder, I had been taught to pronounce a blessing as the Holy Spirit guides my thoughts and feelings. If I feel prompted to do so, I should bless a person to be healed. If not, then I should not. That's simple enough, right?

That's easy to say, but it is not always so easy to put into action.

I thought back a few months to when one of my close friends and his wife conceived twins. Problems arose with the pregnancy and she delivered prematurely, resulting in both of the tiny boys having serious complications. My friend administered blessings to them like any faithful LDS Melchizedek Priesthood holder would, but it was not long before we heard the sad news that one of the twins had passed away. After months in the NICU, the other boy eventually came home and is now growing strong.

I held my fevered son tightly and counted my blessings that my family had never been in such a scary situation. But what if my son's condition had been as serious as with those twin boys? If I am supposed to give a blessing according to the Holy Spirit, and not just according to what *I want* to happen, then how could I know whether my feelings were from inspiration or from my own desires? Clearly, as a father, I would want nothing more in this world than to have my child healthy. If my duty as a priesthood holder was to tune into the frequency of the "Still, Small Voice" prompting me, then how could I possibly tune out the fatherly instincts screaming inside my head?

I soon began to search more diligently for answers, and I kept running into one phrase that gave me a lot of trouble: Blessings are predicated on faith and obedience. Was that supposed to bring me comfort? What did it even mean? To me, that phrase seemed to say that everything should work itself out just fine if I had firm faith in Jesus Christ and I kept my life in accordance with God's commandments. That sounded nice, but my friends with the twins were some of the most faithful and obedient people I knew, and still one of their boys died. Was I to assume their faith was insufficient? Should I have supposed there was something in their personal lives that was blocking them from receiving this blessing?

Some people answer this question by saying that all outcomes are ultimately in God's hands, so if I am not perfectly tuned into the Spirit and I bless someone with something that's not according to God's will ... well, then, God will still carry things out according to *His* plan. Since we are imperfect, that concept rang true to me, but it also left me scratching my head. What was the point of me stressing over giving a priesthood blessing if God would do things His way no matter what I say? If I were on the other end, and someone else was giving me a blessing, did it even matter whether or not I listened to what was said since only God's will mattered and not whatever words were pronounced by the priesthood holder?

This also made me wonder about other blessings that were not meant for the healing of the sick and afflicted—blessings of comfort and guidance. If I were facing a tough decision, what did it matter if I had someone give me a blessing? If my faith and obedience was the key to receiving God's blessings, wouldn't it be just as beneficial to only fast and pray?

In searching for answers to these questions, I spent a lot of time with my nose in the scriptures, listening to LDS General Conference talks, reading blogs, and devouring good books. It seemed like the majority of what I read on the subject of priesthood blessings was dedicated to miracles—the kind where people were able to "arise and walk" after being near death, etc. Many of them said something like, "The power of priesthood blessings is real. Let me tell you about a miracle I witnessed as a result of a priesthood blessing."

I wholeheartedly believe in God showing his divine power by healing people in miraculous ways, but those stories are considered miraculous and special for a reason—they're not how things typically go. It would be easy to have faith in priesthood blessings if everyone were healed instantly every time a blessing was pronounced, but faith is not always that easy.

God teaches us in many ways. Books and messages from general authorities are only some of the ways we learn. Often times, and definitely so in my case, we learn best by experience. I generally understood the words I was studying, but the answers did not really become clear to me until I found myself in one of those dire and scary situations like I mentioned before—the kind that terrified me and tried my soul to the highest level.

Much of this book will be taking you on a personal journey through the two most difficult trials of my life, and by so doing I will show you the answers I received for my questions as well as how they came to me.

I'll tell you right now that, while this book is meant to help build your faith in priesthood blessings, it does not contain any "arise and walk" miracles. Nobody within these pages becomes healed in a way that doctors or scientists are left baffled. The miracles shared in this book are more subtle, but I still see them as miracles nonetheless.

As you read, please keep in mind that what I share are my own thoughts and opinions. I speak only for myself and not for The Church of Jesus Christ of Latter-day Saints or any other organization.

my brothers' hands

Shortly after I returned from serving a mission in Guatemala, on the first Sunday in my new Brigham Young University student ward, a cute girl with curly hair and bright blue eyes caught my attention. I cornered her after the meetings, got her name and apartment number, and we went on our first date two weeks later.

Amber and I dated casually for six months before things began to get serious. After another six months I told her for the first time that I loved her. I did everything the way I was supposed to. I prayed about my decision and the answer was *yes*. I called her father to ask for his blessing, and his answer was also *yes*. I took her to our favorite place at a nearby park, got down on one knee, and asked her to marry me. Her answer was an emphatic *yes*.

Amber was everything to me. I was head-over-heels in love with her.

We were married for time and all eternity a few months later in the Bountiful Utah Temple. As a wedding present, someone gave us access to their timeshare in Puerto Vallarta, Mexico, so even though Amber and I were dirt-poor college students, we spent a week living it up south of the border on our honeymoon.

Everything was perfect until we arrived at the airport to return home. It was easy for me to sense that something was bothering her, but she assured me it was nothing and she would be fine.

Amber's sister had given birth while we were gone, so as soon as we got back to Provo, Amber drove to Wyoming to visit for four days. We called each other constantly while she was gone, and she was once again in great spirits. I assumed that whatever had been bothering her was now behind us, but as soon as she came back to Utah, her mood sank again. We were not fighting, and we were still able to enjoy each other's company, but a gray cloud of gloom hung over her. Two weeks later she decided she needed some time away, and she left to spend a week in Oregon with her father while I stayed in Provo to work. This time she was not quite as happy on the phone, and she was even more glum when she returned.

It was obvious something was wrong, but I was both naïve and optimistic so I underestimated the power depression could have on a person. I loved her. I was willing to do anything for her. So, to me, that meant everything would always work itself out.

One evening I thought I would surprise her with a romantic candlelit dinner. I asked her best friend to invite her over for a few hours, and while they were together I cooked dinner and got out the candlesticks we had bought in

Mexico. I lit the candles a few minutes before expecting her home, but put them out again when an hour passed without any sign of her. I called her friend, but she had no idea where Amber was, saying she had left a long time ago.

More than two hours later Amber came home red-eyed, tired, and shocked that I had been sitting there for so long with dinner on the table. She soon told me that she got into her car and could not stand the thought of coming home, so she turned toward the canyon and just drove around for hours. My timing for a romantic dinner was impeccable since she had spent those hours behind the wheel contemplating whether or not she would leave me. I am not a great cook, and I am even worse at decorating, but my gesture meant the world to her. A few days later she returned the favor, and I came home to a dimly-lit apartment with candles on the table and soft music playing.

For a brief moment it seemed like everything was turning in the right direction, but it did not last. After being married for only a month she told me she had made a big mistake. She said she cared for me as a person, but she did not love me—at least not in the way a wife is supposed to love a husband.

We had known each other for two years now, and we'd had our share of ups and downs while we were dating. Sometimes those downs were connected to me and our relationship, and sometimes they were not. In every instance, though, we had been great at communicating. We had always been able to talk openly about everything. But now—now that we were married—she was a closed book. I tried everything I could think of to open her up, but every time she would just shake her head and say I would not understand.

15

She stayed for another month. I told her multiple times every day that I loved her, but she no longer said it back.

One afternoon while I was at work she called my cell to ask a simple question. Before giving her an answer, I looked at my watch and asked why she was not in class. When she hesitated to answer, I immediately knew something was seriously wrong. I remember that moment as clearly as if it happened to me five minutes ago. I asked, "Are you going somewhere?" Again, she said nothing. I told her to stay put. I would be home in ten minutes.

I quickly found someone to work the rest of my shift, and I sped home to find her standing in the middle of the living room. She held in her hand a note she had written a few days earlier—one that detailed the reasons she needed to leave. She handed it to me and left the room while I read it. In the note she said that none of this was my fault. She did not know when, or even *if* she would come back, but for the time being she needed to be away from me in order to sort her feelings out.

With the note still in my hand, I stood by our living room window and watched her drive away. Amber and I had only been married for two months, and now she was gone.

Within a few minutes my sister-in-law called to ask if everything was all right. She and my brother lived in the same apartment complex, and she had watched Amber drive away with the car packed full. My brother rushed to my apartment. I was sitting on the couch when he walked in, and he asked me what I was going to do now. Up until that moment, I had successfully held in the tears. I hate to cry, and I rarely do. I know other people say it can be a good emotional release, but I hate the feeling of having lost control of my insides. That was exactly what happened—I lost control of my insides. Before I could finish saying, "I don't know," I was bawling uncontrollably. My brother hurdled the coffee table, landed on the sofa next to me, and wrapped his arms tightly around me.

Up until that moment I had never been "held" by one of my brothers before, but that was exactly what I needed. I cried in his arms for about half an hour before I could calm down enough to have a conversation.

When my oldest brother found out, he also rushed over. Before long I was sitting in a chair with their hands upon my head, receiving a priesthood blessing. Apart from wanting Amber to come back, the thing I desired most was to be relieved of my pain. I hurt so much inside that I could barely function. Even with my brothers and other family members there with me, I had never felt so alone in my life.

The priesthood blessing they gave me did not relieve me of that pain. I felt just as rotten after they lifted their hands as I did before. But that does not mean it did nothing for me. Many of the effects that came as a result of that blessing took time.

In the years since, I have looked back on that day and realized just how intimate a priesthood blessing can be. We had secluded ourselves by retreating to an empty room and closing the blinds. The rest of the world did not exist in that moment. And in such an intimate setting, physically feeling the weight of my brothers' hands on my head as they did their best to say what they felt Christ would say if he were there to comfort me, I felt closer to my Savior. I still hurt, mind you, but I felt closer to my big brother, Jesus.

I do remember some of the words from that blessing, which I will talk about later in this book, but even if I could not recall any of it, the experience of the blessing brought me closer to God than if I had been alone in prayer. I had already been spending a lot of time praying about my situation, starting long before Amber left, but this was different.

When I was down on my knees in personal prayer, the only ones involved in that prayer were me, my Father in Heaven, and my mediator, Jesus Christ. When my brothers had their hands placed on my head, I was allowing them into my intimate circle—a circle that I tend to keep very private.

It helped me feel less alone.

three

a father's blessing

My dad found out about Amber leaving me when he got off work, and he immediately called me on the phone. "I'm coming to see you," he said. "I can't let my boy go through something like this without giving him a father's blessing." He left his home in Nevada just after five o'clock, and after nearly a six hour drive he was on my doorstep.

I made no attempt to talk him out of giving me a blessing even though my brothers had already done so earlier in the day. First of all, I could tell how much it meant to him to be able to do this. Secondly, I wanted him to do it. Church leaders have stated that we do not need multiple blessings for the same situation, and it would not be appropriate to go around asking a variety of people for blessings out of a desire to have multiple people administer to me, but this was different.

A father's blessing is a very special thing. In fact, although I cherished the blessing my brothers had given me, if my father had been present at the time, or even if I had known he would be on his way, I would have requested he do it.

Dad got right to it. Within five minutes of arriving at my apartment he had his hands on my head with the shades again drawn for privacy, doing what he called "his duty as a father." After the blessing, we sat on the couch together and he pulled me in close. Like my brother had done earlier in the day, Dad held me in his arms. This time it was different for me, though. Although I very much still hurt inside, the crying had already stopped. I didn't need Dad to hold me until I could stop crying, but it still meant the world to me to have him there. I appreciated his arms around me because *he* was the one who needed to hold me, *his* son. I felt better because I was able to let him share in my pain, and allowing him to do that helped me feel less alone.

My father stayed with me for less than an hour before he was back on the freeway. Late that night he arrived home in time to get three hours of sleep before his alarm clock sounded, announcing that it was time for him to get back to his desk at work.

That, right there, is what I think of when I ponder what it means to take my responsibilities as a priesthood holder seriously. The service my father did for me that day was more important and left a bigger impact on me than anything else he could have done. Priesthood and service go hand-in-hand, and service is about sacrificing time and energy to benefit and love others.

Every day for the previous month I had been feeling unloved as I told my wife I loved her, and she would not say it in return. So, in a time when I was feeling unlovable, my Dad used his priesthood "duty as a father" to prove otherwise.

It is cliché to say that actions speak louder than words, but clichés are clichés for a reason. They're often true. Perhaps the most important thing my father's action did was to show me firsthand how important he thought it was to lean on God during such a hard time. If he had just counseled with me over the phone about the importance and power of prayer, it would not have left as great an impact on my heart.

an answer to a prayer

Priesthood holders are not magicians. Just because they say something does not make it so, even if they have the faith to move mountains. When Christ healed the woman who had an issue of blood, he said, "Be of good comfort. Thy faith hath made thee whole." He said similar words after healing a blind man, and again after healing a leper. Never did Jesus say, "Be of good comfort. *My power* hath made thee whole."

The blessings I had received were very special to me, but now I knew it was my turn to take the reins. It was up to me to take those words to heart and interpret their meaning. Now it was time for *me* to show my faith and act.

Although blessings given to the sick and afflicted are in some ways different from blessings for comfort and guidance, the concept is similar. On page 163 in *Discourses of Brigham Young,* he is quoted as having said this regarding those who ask for blessings over the sick, "Have you used any remedies?" If someone were to say no because they wanted the Elders to lay their hands on them to heal them, he replied, "That is very inconsistent according to my faith. If we are sick, and ask the Lord to heal us, and to do all for us that is necessary to be done, according to my understanding of the Gospel of salvation, I might as well ask the Lord to cause my wheat and corn to grow, without my plowing the ground and casting in the seed. It appears consistent to me to apply every remedy that comes within the range of my knowledge, and to ask my Father in Heaven ... to sanctify that application to the healing of my body."

Whether I need to heal from an ailment, I need guidance, or my soul needs comfort, I still have to do everything in my power to make it happen. The point of a priesthood blessing is not to pave the way for God to take over and do things for me. The point of a blessing is to open the window for God to fill in where my efforts come up short.

I asked my oldest brother to move in with me so I would not have to live alone in my newlywed apartment. I worked extra hard at my job in an effort to feel good about myself and keep depression from overtaking me. I attended the temple often. Those were things I could actually *do*, rather than just sit back in my misery and hope God would take it away.

My little sister is two years younger than I am, and she has always been very protective of me. She checked on me often while I was going through that hard time. One day she asked how I was doing with my personal prayers. I told her how I had been visiting the temple often, sometimes staying in the celestial room longer than I probably should just to stay where I felt close to God. I also said I often poured out my soul in prayer in order to find guidance in such a confusing time.

She asked me if I ever prayed just for comfort and reminded me that the Holy Ghost's role in our lives was not just for guidance, but also to be the Comforter. She told me that the next time I was feeling lonely and lost, that I should pray—but not just a regular prayer. She challenged me to pray *only* for comfort, and to not get off my knees until that comfort came. I had never done that before.

I always felt the loneliest at night. The worst nights of all were when I worked the graveyard shift. At my job I served people with special needs. The people I cared for needed around the clock supervision, even while they were asleep. Once a week it was my responsibility to spend the night on their couch ... awake.

Before Amber left I enjoyed that time alone. I caught up on homework, quietly practiced guitar, read a book, or watched movies. But after she left, even if the TV was on or I had a book in my hands, I mostly sat miserably in my thoughts.

The first time I ever knelt to pray solely for comfort was one of those long nights at work. The pain inside had become so unbearable that I could do little more than stare at the wall and think about how lonely I was. I became determined to stay on my knees until I felt that comfort my sister had talked about. It was not long past midnight when I began praying, and I had the entire night ahead of me.

I poured out my soul. I held nothing back. I talked to my Heavenly Father conversationally, as if I were talking to my earthly father. I began to think of that moment in the book of Luke when Jesus was in the Garden of Gethsemane, feeling overwhelmed as he suffered for our sins. An angel came down and sat with Jesus to strengthen Him. I prayed, "Heavenly Father, I don't know how the whole system works with administering angels, but I could sure use someone here with me. If I could choose who that person might be, I would choose my grandmother, but anyone would be wonderful."

I felt no different for a long time, even after praying specifically for someone to come sit with me, but I was committed to staying at this all night if I needed to.

Then it happened, and it happened suddenly.

I could not see or hear anyone join me in the room, but an overwhelming feeling of love came over me. I still felt the dregs of my pain, mind you, but the feeling of love and companionship was more powerful than anything else inside me. I stopped praying for comfort, and switched to praying only to give thanks to God for what I was experiencing.

I stayed on my knees for a long time, afraid that if I got up I might lose that feeling of comfort I was receiving. After a while, though, I heard one of the special needs girls begin to stir in her bedroom, and I knew I needed to check on her. As I closed my prayer, I pleaded for that comfort to stay with me all night.

It did.

words on my mind

Thinking back to the day Amber left, I have often thought it was interesting that both my brother and father did the same thing as soon as they saw me. They both sat with me on the couch and held me. Neither of them had ever done that before, and neither have done it since. The weight of their hands on my head felt like an extension of that intimate contact.

Hopefully it goes without saying that I am not advocating for that type of physical contact between priesthood holders and those with whom they administer. There's no way I would allow someone from the ward to wrap his arms around me to hold me after I asked for a priesthood blessing. I am just saying that the ritual of laying hands on someone's head carries with it an innate level of intimacy—physical contact.

Many of the miracles Jesus performed involved physical contact. When He appeared on the American continent, He bade the people to come touch Him so that they might know Him and feel connected to Him. He took people by the hand and commanded them to rise. He touched the eyes of the blind man.

As wonderful as that physical connection can be, it is not the only reason God has set forth the ritual of the laying on of hands. If physical contact was all that was important, we would get the same affect by holding hands while we prayed. That was a common custom for some people in Guatemala where I served as a missionary, and it was a beautiful way to feel the Spirit.

A priesthood blessing is different from that. It is different from a typical prayer. The Melchizedek Priesthood holder does not *ask* for blessings, he *pronounces* them. The priesthood holder does not *ask* for guidance, he *gives* guidance.

My brothers and my father pronounced beautiful words in the blessings they gave me. From that point on, it was my responsibility to receive those words. It was my responsibility to exercise my faith in making those blessings happen. It was my responsibility to seek for the interpretation and to understand the meaning behind the counsel given.

The blessing my father gave me left a profound impression on my mind, but now that it has been so many years I only remember his words generally—words of comfort, peace, and strength. I don't remember any phrases specifically. I do remember a specific phrase from my brother though, and I remember it clearly because it was stuck in my mind for a very long time. I pondered over it on a daily basis for months.

"There will come a time when she will realize how much she loves you."

As I pondered those words, I questioned whether or not it was his right to say something like that. Amber had her own agency, and no amount of faith on my part could take that away from her. Could my brother really bless *me* with a blessing that, if I exercised *my* faith, would have the power to make *her* remember how much she loved me?

It took me quite a while to sort that question out. After all, I did feel the spirit as he said those words, but I also knew the reality of the Plan of Salvation, which hinges on everyone's own agency to choose.

The answer to the first question—the one about whether or not it was his right to say those words—was yes. It was within his rights, and I believe he was guided by the spirit when he said them.

The answer to the second question—the one about whether or not someone could bless me in such a way that could cause her to remember her love for me—was no. A blessing on *my* head could not cause *her* mind to shift.

That may sound confusing, but it made sense to me when I really came to understand his words. He was not blessing me that she would come back to me. He was giving me words of guidance. He was giving me words that I could hang on to for comfort. In essence, he was not saying something that would require her loss of agency in order for it to come true. He was giving me a prophetic tool I could carry with me through the hard times.

That realization begged another question. Isn't that sort of like using the priesthood power to tell the future? Can someone really do that?

The scriptures are full of prophets and seers using their calling and priesthood to receive revelation for the world. Many of those revelations are prophetic in nature. Samuel the Lamanite climbed the city wall to not only proclaim repentance, but to also foretell the coming of the Lord. Joseph Smith envisioned the future spreading of the gospel when he proclaimed that "... the truth of God will go forth boldly, nobly, and independent until it has penetrated every continent ..."

It would not have been my brother's right to receive revelation for the whole world since his calling was not to be the world's prophet, but he was well within his right to receive prophetic revelation in that priesthood blessing—revelation for that individual—for me.

But how could I know whether or not he was speaking from divine inspiration, or whether his words came from his own desires? There was no easy way for me to answer that question, but that was where my faith would need to come in.

The concept was the same as when I had received my patriarchal blessing years before. It was up to me to decide how to receive those words, and what I would do with them. It was up to me to find interpretation of them. Many of the promises in my patriarchal blessing have already come to pass. Some of those blessings are specific, and others are general. I have studied and cherished my patriarchal blessing ever since I received it, and I have tried to take it to heart. Some of my interpretations from it have happened how I expected them to, but other things have occurred differently than what I was anticipating.

My patriarchal blessing is a tool and a guide I get to take with me everywhere throughout my life, and the blessing from my brother had the potential to be the same. It was up to me to seek the interpretation of his words and to press forward in faith in that direction.

six

not yet

For a while after Amber left, we talked on the phone every day—often times more than once a day. Every time we spoke I told her I loved her, and every time I said those words I heard nothing in response. That silence hurt every time. Instead of getting accustomed to it, the pain increased every time it happened.

We started out talking every day, but after a few weeks we started to skip a day here and there. By the time she had been gone a few months, the frequency of our conversations dwindled down to three or four times a week. It wasn't that I cared for her any less or that I grew bored talking to her, but I got to the point where I would pace for half an hour or more with the phone in my hand, trying to will myself into dialing her number. Some days I simply lacked the strength to make that call, and I would end up sticking my cell phone back into my pocket to avoid the pain. Those days became more common the more I heard silence after I said, "I love you."

She eventually stopped being silent, and began to say things like, "You keep waiting for me to say it back, but that's not going to happen."

She got a job. She started making long term plans in Oregon. I began to doubt she would ever come back.

Some of my friends advised me it was time to consider making that difficult decision and thinking about moving on without her in my life. I couldn't bear the thought. "Not yet," I would say. "Not until I've tried everything in my power."

I had been meeting often with my bishop. He was the bishop of the family ward Amber and I had attended together, and I continued to counsel with him regularly even after my rental agreement expired and I moved out of the ward. When he said he thought it was time to consider moving on, I shook my head and said, "Not yet."

When my mother told me it was time to consider divorce, I prayed over that decision in the temple, but I still felt like Amber was going to one day realize she loved me and would come rushing back to me—just like my brother had said in the blessing. The answer I received in the temple was again, "Not yet" and I resolved to fight some more.

It was on my birthday that I finally lost my last bit of hope. All month, whenever Amber and I talked on the phone, she would ask what I wanted for my birthday and I always said the same thing. I wanted her permission to come see her in Oregon. It didn't need to be a long visit, and I could even stay at my aunt's house ten miles away. I just wanted to see her.

I had been asking this of her for a long time, and I hoped she would give in now that it was my birthday. Over and over she told me she would think about it. When my birthday finally came and she chose to give me a gift certificate to the guitar store instead, I knew I had her answer and I knew my last bit of hope was gone.

There was nothing left inside of me at that point. My emotions and self-worth had been whittled down to zero, and I had tried everything I could think of. I resigned myself to the thought that the day would never come when she would realize how much she loved me. I cried harder that day than any other day of my life—including the day she left.

seven

single awareness day

I had no interest in dating after the divorce, so it didn't even dawn on me that it was February 14th until my Sociology professor greeted the class with the words, "Happy Single Awareness Day." I laughed along with everyone else, but from that point on I spent the day wallowing in the fact that I was alone on Valentine's Day.

Amber had moved back to Provo by this time in order to continue her schooling, but we had kept our lives separate—for the most part. Out of more than thirty thousand students walking around campus, she seemed to be the person I bumped into the most.

As if Single Awareness Day wasn't already enough to make me think about Amber all day, something happened that afternoon that forced me to think about her even more. I had arrived early to class and found a campus newspaper sitting on my desk. Halfway down the front page my eye was drawn to a large photograph with Amber's name printed underneath, giving her credit as the photographer. This was a big deal. She was both a writer and a photographer, and it had been her long-time goal to write for the paper and get one of her photos on the front page.

I got absolutely nothing out of the professor's lecture that hour because I spent the whole time debating whether or not to send her a congratulatory email. Although we had been keeping our distance—keeping our level of contact limited only to the times we saw each other on campus—I decided to go ahead and send her a quick message. While still sitting in class, I sent a single sentence note to her email account, and that was it. I checked randomly throughout the day, but I got no response until late that night.

About an hour before I was going to go to bed she replied, but rather than just saying "thanks" and "hope you are well," she asked if I would be willing to come to her apartment to give her a priesthood blessing. That was not at all what I expected her to say, and although it was unusual for her to request something like this, I still cared about her, so I agreed.

She gave me her address, and I drove there to find her alone in her living room. As I suspected, her Valentine's Day was as terrible as mine, and she told me she could really use a priesthood blessing to help her find comfort. She had spent all evening considering who to ask and decided I was the only one who had a clue what she was going through.

This was really interesting to me for a few reasons. First of all, the whole time we were married I tried and tried to get her to open up, but she always told me I "just wouldn't understand." Now she felt I was the only person who would. Secondly, she had never requested a priesthood blessing from me before—not while we were dating or even during her hardest times while we lived together.

We had the living room to ourselves, so we talked for about an hour before I gave her the blessing. We then sat and talked some more.

The purpose of the visit had nothing to do with re-kindling our relationship. That didn't even come up in con-versation, but we talked about everything else. She was able to open up to me again in a way she had not been able to the entire time we were married. We sat face-to-face in conversa-tion the whole night, up until it was time for her to get ready to go to class in the morning.

I spent the rest of the week processing the complicat-ed things we had discussed. A week later she called and asked if she could come over and see me again. This time it was much earlier in the evening. We talked in my apartment for about six hours—until about three o'clock in the morning. Just like before, the purpose of the visit was just to talk, not to fix our relationship in order to rekindle what we once had.

At the most intimate part of our conversation she not only apologized for everything she had put me through, but she also told me she loved me. She said she had always loved me, even during the times when she said otherwise.

Our conversation eventually slowed to the point where we were both sitting in silence. I noticed that she had fallen asleep, but I didn't bother to wake her. For the rest of the night I didn't move a muscle out of fear that I might awaken her. I sat silently watching the clock. My mind reverted back to my brother's words. He had been right. The day did come when she realized how much she loved me.

But why had he felt prompted to say that in the blessing? It didn't save my marriage. It didn't even really help me know what to do.

I was able to realize it was important because those words were a tool that helped me carry on—even during my darkest times. They gave me hope when most of me wanted to throw in the towel. Even when I decided it was time to move on with my life and I thought my brother's words had been a mistake, I was glad he and the Lord had given them to me.

The most difficult thing I have had to deal with since ending that marriage has been to constantly wonder if I truly tried hard enough to keep it together. If I had not had that hope, I'm afraid to think I might have given up too early, and I would have had to live with that for the rest of my life.

I do feel my brother was inspired when he said those words. I took those words to mean something, and although things did not happen the way I was expecting or hoping they would, they still happened.

I will always be grateful for those words.

eight

to suffer

I mentioned earlier that I had prayed about my decision to marry Amber, and I got an answer to my prayer. I felt very strongly that I had God's blessing. I also felt I did everything I could to make it work. If God knows the beginning from the end, why did He give me His blessing to marry Amber when He knew it was going to fall apart?

Let me first answer that question by backtracking and asking another question: What's the purpose of this life? It is a complicated question that Latter-day Saints love to offer simple answers to. One of the most common responses is that we are here to be tested and to prove ourselves. Other people say we are here to gain experience in order to learn. I strongly prefer the "gain experience" answer over the "tested" answer, but they're both right.

Suffering helps us appreciate joy. Adam and Eve felt no joy in the Garden of Eden because they had not learned what it was like to suffer any form of discomfort. The more we learn to rise above our suffering, the more we can embrace true joy.

To live is to suffer, but suffering in itself does not make us better or worse. We feel pain for a reason. It motivates us to move and change. We want to find a way to escape the hurt. It causes us to make decisions, and as we choose our actions, we choose what path to follow in life. Thus, suffering pushes us to become someone we would not otherwise be.

Nobody on earth is exempt from this, not even the best people. Joseph Smith's life was riddled with suffering and trials, which made it possible for God to teach and mold him into who he needed to be. Martin Luther, Abraham Lincoln, Martin Luther King Jr.—it seems like all of those who have been an influence for good have suffered in ways that dwarf my own problems. Jesus was pure and strong, and although He was the only one born to this world who lived a sinless life, He suffered more than any of us—more than we can even comprehend. He was able to rise above all, and that's what we also need to learn to do.

If we suffer, but fail to rise above our trials, then the best we could hope for would be to remain the same. The worst, and most probable thing that would happen to someone who fails to rise above their pain, would be that their suffering would turn them into a bitter person. We came to earth to have the opportunity to better ourselves. If we look at life through the lens of gaining experience in order to learn, we are better capable of using our sufferings to become stronger and happier people.

I have heard it said that everything happens for a reason. Sometimes that reason is because we're stupid and make poor decisions. How true that is! It is my opinion that God does not punish us by making bad things happen to us. He does not strike us with lightning because we are thinking bad thoughts. We might, on the other hand, get struck by lightning if we walk around a golf course in a thunderstorm holding a golf club above our head. That's not God striking us down. That is suffering the natural consequences of our actions.

To be a little more serious, if I smoke a pack of cigarettes every day for fifty years and I get lung cancer, then that's not God giving me lung cancer. I did that to myself. If I text while I drive and I crash, that's not God punishing me. If I drop out of high school and I can't find a good job ... you get the picture.

God's punishment, if you want to call it that, is more subtle. He withdraws His Spirit and influence from us when we are not living worthy of it. Some people say God doesn't do that, but we withdraw *ourselves* from His influence. However you want to look at it, the result is the same.

Suffering does not only come as a result of bad choices, though. Sometimes bad things happen to us even when we're being good people, which can sometimes make us think we're being punished for something. Again, nobody was better than Jesus, and bad things happened to Him all the time. We need to stop asking ourselves, "What did I do to deserve this?" and start asking, "What does God want me to learn from this?"

Whether our suffering is a result of bad decisions, or whether something terrible has happened to us and there was nothing we could do to prevent it, we still have the ability to choose whether our experiences will embitter us or bring us closer to God.

Now I can answer the question I posed earlier about Amber. If God knew my marriage to Amber would fall apart, and I was doing my best to be a good person, then why did He give me His blessing to marry her? Is God sadistic that way? The answer is no. Quite the opposite, actually. He loved me enough to let me suffer in order to give me an opportunity to grow.

The responsibility of making a decision about whether or not to marry Amber was my own. It's not proper to ask God to decide things for us. I prayed about our relationship all along the way, and when I brought my biggest decision before God, I was not asking Him to tell me what to do. I was asking him if my decisions were in line with what He had in store for me and my life, and they were.

I was twenty-three when I married Amber, and that was the first time in my life I had ever suffered that deeply. Sure, I'd had some trying times before. One of my best friends died when I was eighteen from a swimming accident. I had been to the emergency room twice. But this was the first time I suffered to that extent. And for the first time in my life I learned what it was like to truly *need* to lean on my Brother and Savior, Jesus Christ, for support. I was broken down so low that I could not stand on my own, and through it all there was only one place I could find peace.

Because Christ has suffered all things, He was able to give me the peace and comfort I needed. He not only took upon Himself the sins of the world, but also all the pain, sorrows, and suffering we experience. I truly felt like Christ understood me when I was humble enough to lean on him— to place my burdens upon Him.

Feeling so low made me more humble, and being more humble helped me see the bigger picture, especially after time went by and I was able to look back on what I had gone through. My experience brought me closer to Christ. I was able to feel Him near me when I needed it, and I was able to see His hand in my life. That experience will always be a part of my testimony that I cannot deny. There have been times in my life when my testimony has been tried, but that period surrounding my divorce has always served as an anchor. How could I ever deny Christ's love when I felt Him so near during those lonely times?

My experience with Amber gave me the opportunity to learn how to move away from misery. I could have shaken my fist at the heavens and carried a grudge against Amber and God for the rest of my life, but I didn't. Now I look back on that period of my life with a smile. The pain I experienced did not dissipate as soon as the marriage was over. I suffered for years because of it. But as painful as it was, I was able to eventually rise above that suffering. I like who I have become, and I would not be who I am now without that period in my life.

Oftentimes, as God's children, we come running to Him to relieve us of our hard times. The good news is that God will always be there, and He will always help us. But that does not mean our relief will necessarily come the way we want it to. While I was going through those difficult times, there were moments when I pleaded with God to take it all away. He was there to hold me up and let me lean on Him for support, which helped make my pain bearable, but He did not take the trial or my pain away completely.

When it comes down to it, God and I have the same goal for my life. We both want me to be happy, and I'm a happier person because of my experience with Amber. To live is to suffer. To suffer is to be given the opportunity to choose which path we want to take, and who we want to become.

nine

starting over

I had a hard time moving on with my life after our divorce was final, but that was exactly what I needed to do. Although I thought I was hot stuff when I was younger and had dated regularly since I was sixteen, it took me a long time to become interested in having a relationship. I eventually moved off campus into a house with some friends, and after about a year-and-a-half hiatus I jumped back into the dating pool. My first relationship lasted a month. My next made it to three months. Then I dated a girl for a year and a half before realizing there was no future there.

The house my friends and I had been living in was sold, and we were forced to find a new place. We all moved together across town, and on my first Sunday in our new ward I saw Grace for the first time. With her long blonde hair and bright green eyes, I could not stop staring at her. I knew I had to meet this girl, and by the end of the day I had her cornered by the drinking fountain.

Call it destiny, divine intervention, or just plain luck, but the timing was impeccable. She had just moved to town from Wyoming and was staying with her parents while she looked for an apartment. If she had arrived two weeks earlier, or if I had moved into the neighborhood two weeks later, we would not have met before she found her new place.

We hit it off from the very first moment. On our first date we got sandwiches at Quiznos and watched *Napoleon Dynamite* in the theater, and we started spending every day together from that day forward. Two weeks later she came home to Nevada with me to meet my parents. Another week after that I was sitting nervously in front of her father to ask his blessing to marry her. Having already been married in the temple once, I had to get permission from the LDS First Presidency to do it again, but that didn't take long, and Grace and I were married for time and all eternity in the Jordan River Temple just three and a half months after we met. She is the most wonderful thing to have ever happened to me.

It took me another year and a half to finish college, and then a job opportunity brought us to Idaho where we later started our own business.

We tried for six years to have children, but after many visits to fertility specialists nobody could tell us why we were not able to conceive. Infertility was both sad and frustrating, but those ill feelings soon turned to excitement when we decided to adopt. We adopted a baby boy from Mississippi and seventeen months later a baby girl from Idaho.

About six months shy of our ten year wedding anniversary, we were able to make the last payment on one of our business loans. We still had some student loans and another business loan to pay off, but we were able to take a step back and look at how far we had come. We were far from rich, but the business was rolling along now. We had the two most beautiful children in the world. And best of all, we had each other. We were even more in love coming up on our tenth anniversary than we had ever been.

On that day, after we had made the last payment on that big loan, I remember driving together late at night talking about how lucky we were. Our biggest stress had always been money, and since we had worked so hard together, spent very little on frivolities, and didn't fight over finances, we were conquering our biggest trial. We were living the dream, but only days after that last payment was made, something very serious happened to shake up our picture perfect life.

ten

something is wrong

Grace and I both started feeling sick about the same time. She developed a cough and I got a nasty head cold. There was no reason to be alarmed. This sort of thing happened all the time, but within a few days I was feeling better and Grace was feeling worse. By the time I was back to normal, Grace was having a tough time getting out of bed and she coughed nonstop.

I felt so bad for her. A few years earlier I had contracted bronchitis, and it took me about four months to stop coughing. I thought I knew what she was going through, but she soon began to have symptoms that were completely foreign to anything I had experienced. All of her joints, especially her wrists and ankles, began to cause her significant pain, sometimes seizing up. She could not get her fever to come down, and her entire body ached.

When she finally decided she was not getting anywhere with any over-the-counter medications, she tried to get an appointment with our family doctor. There were no openings on the day she called, so she went to the Instacare Clinic.

Neither of us thought much about the visit. We both assumed she would see a doctor for fifteen minutes, get a prescription for an antibiotic, and she would be back home resting in no time. While she was waiting for the doctor, though, she noticed one of her ankles was swollen. She knew she had not done anything to hurt it, so she brought it to the doctor's attention, and he insisted she go to the emergency room. He was worried she may have a blood clot.

Grace called me at work and we discussed our options. This was the last thing we wanted. I was convinced the doctor was trying to pawn the responsibility of diagnosis onto someone else. We thought she had bronchitis, or something similar—but a blood clot? That did not make any sense. We decided to call our family doctor before making any decisions, and he said, "If he thinks there's a possibility of a blood clot, then that's not something you gamble with."

Ugh. Now it sounded like our family doctor was also trying to pawn responsibility off to an ER doctor as well. We had just finished paying off that big loan, and a trip to the ER was going to be much more expensive than what we expected to pay in order to get Grace feeling better. Still, we knew what we had to do, and Grace's health was obviously more important than money.

Grace texted me throughout the day as the emergency room continually added on to the list of expensive tests they wanted to perform. The results of a blood test raised a few red flags but did not provide anything conclusively.

Some x-rays came next, which helped rule out the blood clot, but now they were worried about something else. She texted me again before going in to have a CT scan, and then I didn't hear anything else from her until she came home.

She walked through the door with red eyes and a stack of papers in her hands. It was obvious she had been crying, so I held out my arms and waved for her to come to me. She buried her head into my chest and cried some more. She then began to tell me that they found some scary things during the CT scan. She showed me the stack of papers, which explained the two most likely diagnoses.

One possible diagnosis was sarcoidosis. I had never heard of that one before, so I didn't know if it should scare me or not. The other possibility was lymphoma. That one I had heard of, and I knew that was a form of cancer, so that one did scare me ... sort of. I mean, it should have scared me, but it didn't really sink in at first. As she continued to cry on my shoulder, I was more worried about her emotional state than I was about her physical health. It was not that I didn't take the diagnosis seriously, but it just did not make sense. Eight hours ago she went in to get some antibiotics for what I thought was bronchitis, and now they were thinking she might have cancer?

I held her as she cried, trying to find the right words to console her. The only thing I could think of was that I was sure it was not cancer. It had to be something else—maybe it was that sarco-whatever-it's-called. Maybe it wasn't even that. Maybe it was still just a bad case of bronchitis or something. We scheduled an appointment to see a specialist, but that would not take place for two more days. We would have to wait until then to know anything more.

finding the right words

Grace expressed a desire to receive a priesthood blessing regarding her health issues. The LDS church's Melchizedek Priesthood *Administering the Church* handbook states that two Melchizedek priesthood holders should participate whenever possible, so I asked Grace who she wanted to come assist me. She chose Jack, who was one of our home teachers as well as a good friend. He anointed her with the oil. I sealed the anointing and pronounced a blessing upon her head.

I must admit something regarding the blessing. It was hard for me to know what to say in that blessing because I still didn't know what I was dealing with.

I have heard some men say they completely clear their mind before giving a blessing because they do not want their own opinions and desires to cloud their ability to receive inspiration. I can see why some would say that, and that was how I was taught. In the past, whenever I caught myself planning beforehand something I might say, I would quickly shake it from my mind and remind myself that I needed to give the blessing from inspiration.

I don't do it that way anymore, though. At some point I came to realize that inspiration can come at any time—whether that be at the moment my hands were on someone's head, or if it came hours before.

I now believe in preparing myself beforehand as much as possible. Unless I'm called upon to give a blessing without any notice, I like to remove myself to say a personal prayer to prepare myself mentally and spiritually. Although it does not always come while I'm alone in prayer, I have found that is an ideal moment to listen for inspiration. Sometimes I also pray with the person receiving the blessing before I lay my hands on their head.

I have received inspiration at various times throughout my life. It does not only come while I'm on my knees in prayer. We have been commanded to keep a prayer in our heart when we are not kneeling in formal prayer. This means we establish a connection with God while we have our head bowed, and we keep that connection throughout the day, even while we go about our normal business. If we keep this connection strong, then there's no reason inspiration cannot come at any moment. Why would it be any different while preparing for a blessing? If I connect my heart with God, and I feel His inspiration while I'm at the breakfast table spooning Cheerios into my mouth, then, to me, that's as wonderful as if it were to happen while I'm halfway through the blessing.

Also, I think it is beautiful to think of myself as God's mouthpiece, or as a tool in God's hands, while I'm performing an ordinance, but I think of those terms differently than some people do. When I think of a tool, I sometimes think of something like a hammer. I think of something that just sits there and waits for someone to put it to good use. But I'm not a hammer. I'm not inanimate. God created me in His image. He gave me a brain so that I might think things through. He gave me a spirit so that I might connect with others. I am a tool in God's hands when I take my heart, might, mind, and strength, and I dedicate them to doing what I feel is asked of me.

But how could I do that with Grace's blessing when I didn't know what I was dealing with? How could I prepare myself to receive inspiration if I had no idea whether she had cancer or a bad cold? I felt like I was in the dark. I felt restless trying to prepare my mind. It would have been easy to bless her with a speedy recovery if I knew she had a cold. It does not require a lot of faith to bless someone to get better from something they would likely overcome in a few days anyway. But cancer—that would be a whole different ball game. Not everyone gets over lymphoma.

I prayed for inspiration and I kept my heart connected to God throughout the day, but when the time came for me to give the blessing my mind was still blank. Jack and I placed our hands on Grace's head, and I began pronouncing the blessing without any idea of what to say. I prayed within my heart that God would speak through me, and He did just that.

Even though I was the person saying the words, I took a step back in my mind and listened to the words as if I were an outsider listening in. This blessing belonged to Grace, but it affected me too. I didn't know if the words "speedy recovery" would come out of my mouth, or even "eventual recovery." In the end, I never said anything about the recovery. I simply did not feel promptings of the Spirit to tell her she would recover, but I also knew that did not mean she wouldn't. It just meant I did not feel inspired to say it.

I felt a warm comfort reassuring me that everything was going to be okay. But just what "okay" meant, I didn't know. I had already learned in the past that being "okay" did not necessarily mean I wasn't about to go through something difficult.

One part of the blessing really stood out to me. I said she would see special miracles along this journey if she was willing to look for them. That part stood out to me for a few different reasons. Obviously, it was nice to know God had some miracles in store for us. When I thought of miracles received by sick people, I initially thought that meant she would get better, but that was not what I said in the blessing. I said she would see them "if she was willing to look for them." I took that to mean that *we both* should be looking for them since we would be going through this together, and if we had to look for them, then it stood to reason that those miracles were not likely to be the obvious "Rise, take up thy bed, and walk" type of miracles we've all heard about. These miracles were likely to be more subtle.

Those words stuck with me for a long time, and I have come to realize that there are many instances in the scriptures when similar words have been spoken. As God's children, we have the right to ask for miracles. That's one of the ways God shows His hand in our lives. That's what it means for Him to open the "... windows of heaven, and pour you out a blessing, that there shall not be room enough to receive it."

God wants us to ask Him for blessings. To me, that means He *wants* us to ask for miracles, but we do not have the right to demand what those miracles might be. We do not get to say, "I want a specific miracle, and that is the only miracle I'm willing to accept." We need to keep our eyes open for whatever miracles He has in store for us. If we do that, we'll see them. I know that's true because my wife and I put that idea to the test and we began to see miracles all along the way—some of them subtle, and others more obvious.

twelve

eyes open for subtle miracles

Grace and I were glad to be able to get an appointment with a specialist so quickly. Our first visit with him was just a consultation, but it meant a lot more to me than that. Even though he would not be doing anything other than looking at the CT scan and x-rays from the emergency room, I was somehow convinced that he would put my mind at ease. I was sure he would look everything over and tell us the emergency room staff did not know what they were talking about. After all, they were emergency room staff, not specialists. They couldn't possibly know everything about everything, right?

One of the first things the doctor did was to pull up the CT scan on the computer screen and discuss the problem areas. The images all looked like blobs to me, but as he pointed and spoke, he confirmed everything that the ER doctor had said was correct. There was always a small possibility it was something else, but he was almost certain it was either sarcoidosis or lymphoma.

My stomach turned as he spoke. I'm not sure if I was being optimistic or just naïve up until that point, but it was not until we were sitting in that specialist's office that reality finally set in. This was serious. This type of thing did not happen only other people. This was happening to us.

The two likely diagnoses, sarcoidosis and lymphoma, both looked the same on a scan. There was no way of knowing which it was until they could do a biopsy. That meant they would have to stick a tube down her throat, and then insert something down that tube with a tiny camera to take samples of the lymph nodes in her chest.

This doctor preferred to keep his patients awake during the procedure, which worried Grace. She could not go twenty seconds without coughing her lungs out. How could she possibly sit through something like that for an hour?

As much as she dreaded the thought of the procedure, we were relieved to find he had an opening in his schedule the following Monday. We had been led to believe it would take weeks to get the procedure scheduled, so we considered ourselves very lucky.

Once we were in the parking lot, right when we were about to get into the car to leave, a thought popped into Grace's mind. She ran back inside and asked the front desk lady to double check our insurance to make sure we were covered. After a few minutes and a few phone calls to the insurance agency, we realized that this doctor was no longer covered by our insurance. The whole insurance world had become a lot more complicated with recent health care law changes, and the receptionist failed to make sure everything was good-to-go. We had come to this particular specialist because this was where the emergency room staff told us to go.

My mind immediately remembered the blessing I had given Grace the day before, counseling her to look for miracles along the way. Checking on the insurance felt like one of those. It was not a life-changing miracle, but it left an impression on our minds.

We had been worrying about Grace's procedure. Our minds had been fixated on the possibility of her needing chemotherapy treatments. We were becoming increasingly more worried about the worst-case scenarios. We had not been thinking about insurance matters or whether the emergency room had sent us to the right specialist.

The lady at the front desk had everything lined up for the procedure, and she had already allowed us to have a consultation with this doctor, which we ultimately had to pay out of our own pocket. The procedure would have taken place on the next business day, and if the error had not been caught by then, that would have crippled us financially— even more than we already were.

The thought seemed to have popped into Grace's mind out of nowhere. It felt like a little reminder that God was looking out for us. It was the kind of miracle we might often overlook.

thirteen

searching for answers

The next few weeks were very difficult for our family. Every day reality sank in more and more, and every day my wife got sicker and sicker. She coughed deeper and more frequently. Her joints gave her so much pain that she could hardly move at times. Her body hurt so much that it was a struggle just to go from lying in bed to lying on the couch to watch the kids.

Every morning I felt guilty when I left for work—leaving Grace in such a state. I'm self employed, so I do not earn an hourly wage. The amount of time I have to put in depends on how much work comes in that week. I do not come home until I finish everything on my to-do list.

Even though my goal was always to hurry through my workload so I could get back to my wife and kids, my mind was so consumed that I could never seem to get out of first gear. I tried, but I worked so slowly that I was usually late, even when I didn't have a lot to do.

* * *

It took another two weeks to get a consultation with a new specialist. He knew we had already sat through one with the other specialist, so he was willing to do our consultation on the same day as the procedure.

He sat down with us for about half an hour and discussed everything that needed to be done. I still held on to a tiny bit of hope that this new specialist would see something different in the CT scan, like there was still a chance it was just bronchitis or something, but that did not happen. He confirmed everything the other doctors said.

One thing that made this doctor different from the first specialist was that he insisted on having Grace asleep during the process. What a relief!

The anesthesiologist came in, administered some knock-out medicine, and they wheeled Grace off to the biopsy room. As they were leaving, the doctor turned to me and said the procedure would take forty-five minutes to an hour.

About a week before the appointment, I began to realize how intense my anxiety would likely be as I waited for her procedure to finish, so I spent hours in my recording studio. I recorded guitars, bass guitars, drums, and vocals onto my laptop so I could take it with me to the hospital. My hope was that—since recording music was one of my favorite hobbies—taking time to mix the audio tracks would help keep my mind off the intensity of the situation.

Having my laptop with me did no good at all. I sat alone in Grace's hospital room awaiting her return, not knowing quite how long it would take, and not knowing what the doctor would tell us when he did come back. I found myself staring blankly for the first twenty minutes, hurting more and more as time went on. I tried to will myself into playing with the music on my laptop, but I just could not get myself to do it.

I soon realized there were only two things I could do to keep myself from staring blankly at the floor—reading my scriptures and praying. I would read for a bit, pray for a few minutes, read, pray, read, and pray. Attempting anything else was useless.

As I prayed, I pleaded with my Heavenly Father to send someone to sit with me—much like I had done on that difficult night years before while I was going through hard times with Amber. I wish I could say I felt that same intense relief, but I didn't this time. It was not that I felt abandoned—quite the contrary, actually. I felt like I was being accompanied in my trial, but I also felt like there was a reason for me to experience this pain, and the best I could do was to lean on my relationship with God.

I pled with God, "Please. I know this life is about trials and experience, but I can't handle this. I can't live without her. Please don't ask me to do this."

For the first forty-five minutes, I could not help but look up at the clock every four or five minutes. Now that I knew they could return at any moment, I began to look up every two minutes. Once a full hour passed, my heart started to race, and I began to sweat like I had just finished an intense workout, but they still did not return.

An hour and fifteen minutes went by without any word, so I decided to walk to the drinking fountain. My legs felt like rubber and my head was light. I worried I was about to pass out.

An hour and a half came and went as I continued to read, pray, read, and pray.

An hour and forty-five minutes passed, and I began to assume the worst—that something had gone seriously wrong. I tried not to think about what that might mean, but I could not keep my mind from going there. The doctor had sounded so confident that he would be back in an hour or less with an answer.

The doctor finally stuck his head into the room after two hours. Sensing my anguish, he assured me that Grace was okay, and he would be in to talk to us after Grace was awake. They kept her somewhere else in the hospital while she continued to sleep, and I stayed another half hour alone in my misery.

Once Grace was again coherent, they wheeled her back into the room with me. I pulled my chair up next to her. We held hands and waited for the doctor to return.

"I wish I could tell you I have good news ...," he said. My stomach turned and my heart sank, but he continued on. "... but I don't have any bad news either." He went on to tell us that it is very rare for this to happen, but the results of the biopsy were inconclusive. He usually took six samples from someone's chest during this procedure, but he took twenty from Grace. That was why it took so long.

We would now need to try a different procedure— a different kind of biopsy. This one would require a different doctor—a surgeon—to make an incision just above her sternum and go directly in through her chest.

We continued to talk about diagnosis possibilities, but the doctor could not answer many of our questions. As badly as we wanted answers, anything he said on the matter would only be speculation, so he would not tell us.

Grace spent the rest of the day recovering in bed while I did my best to keep the kids out of the bedroom. I took my own temperature and discovered that I now had a fever of 101 degrees. I felt terrible, and I knew my reason for feeling this way was from stress. I learned firsthand where the phrase "worried myself sick" had come from.

That night, as Grace and I were talking, she said with tears in her eyes, "I think it's time we start accepting the fact that this is probably cancer." I had been thinking the same thing. As much as the doctor had tried to hide his opinion, we could both tell by the way he talked that he believed it was the worst case scenario—lymphoma.

fourteen

don't leave us

The next few weeks were worse than any before. My fever came down by the next morning, but I moved slower than ever at work. I could not eat. I lost twelve pounds in just seven days, which meant I had even less energy and moved even slower at work.

Time was not our friend. The more time passed, the worse Grace felt. Her lungs, her joints, her body—everything hurt. The more time passed, the more she longed to just be able to do her basic motherly duties again.

One evening she decided to push through her pain in order to give our two kids a bath. I was busy in the kitchen when I heard her calling for me. I could tell by the tone of her voice that she was in serious pain and was crying. I came running and found her on her back in the middle of the hallway. At first I thought she had fallen and hurt herself, but that was not it.

71

She had started to feel exhausted from bathing the kids, and since they were not ready to get out quite yet, she decided to lie down in the hall to rest a moment. When she felt they had been in long enough, she then realized she could not move. Her joints had seized up.

I had to pick her up and carry her back to bed. I got the kids dried off and into their pajamas, and then went back in to lie with her for a while. I never could find the right words to say in moments like that as she sobbed into my shoulder.

As much as she was hurting, Grace worried more about us than she did about herself. It tore her apart to think that I might be left without her—especially after everything I had gone through years ago with Amber. She knew my past experiences had already left me with an ongoing fear about losing those I love.

She worried about our kids, who were only three and four years old. Would they even remember her if she died? For the most part, we tried our best to help the little ones live their normal, innocent lives. There was no way to pretend Mommy was not sick, but we avoided any discussions about death with the kids, at least until we could know for certain what was going on. But kids seem to have a sense for these kinds of things, no matter how young.

We heard our three-year-old daughter, Macie, crying one night in bed. She had only been in her room with the lights off for a few minutes. We rushed in to see what the matter was. She latched onto Grace's neck and would not let go. "Mommy, don't leave us. Don't leave us," she cried over and over.

Grace carried her out to the living room, and they sat together in the rocking chair—the same chair Grace used to sit in while rocking her to sleep when she was brand new. I sat on the couch nearby and watched them both cry bitterly. There was not much else I could do. Macie repeated those words over and over for half an hour, "Mommy, don't leave us. Don't leave us." We tried to ask her what she meant, and we tried to redirect her mind, but that was all she said for half an hour. "Mommy, don't leave us. Don't leave us."

It tore me apart.

bringing dad along

A week and a half passed after Grace's first biopsy before we were finally able to sit down with the surgeon for a consultation, and then it was another five days before the actual surgery.

My last experience at the hospital had humbled me completely. I had gone in thinking I could handle being alone, only to find out it pushed my emotions well past what I thought possible—to the point that my physical body suffered. I was not going to make that mistake again.

I needed someone to be there with me. I needed someone to talk to and keep my mind from going to dark places, so the first thing I did was to ask my father to come along. He and Mom now lived in Idaho, and although they lived in a different city, they were close enough that I knew I could count on him to be available for support.

The second thing I did was to request a blessing. As miserable and overwhelmed as I had been over the last six weeks, this was the first time I asked for one. Even when Jack, our home teacher, came before the first biopsy to help me administer to Grace, I made the conscious decision not to ask for one.

I don't know why I'm like that. I don't know why it is so hard for me to ask—like I'm admitting my weakness or something. I believe fervently in the power of the priesthood and the laying on of hands, and I'm always willing to administer to someone else if I'm called upon. I'm also not afraid to humble myself in personal prayer, but for some reason I'm very slow to request a priesthood blessing for myself.

I'm glad Jack did not try to push me into receiving a blessing a few weeks earlier. I knew he would have been willing if I had wanted one. That was exactly his role—to be willing. The Melchizedek Priesthood *Administering the Church* handbook states, "Brethren should administer to the sick at the request of the sick person ... so the blessing will be according to their faith." I think this statement would also apply to someone like me who was not sick, but still needed to be administered to.

Why is that? Why is it important for the sick person to ask?

At any point during this hard time, if someone were to ask me whether or not I believed in priesthood blessings, I would have emphatically said *yes*! I believed, but it still took me a long time to ask, and faith is more than just believing. Faith drives our belief to action. I'm glad Jack did not push me into receiving a blessing because it gave me time to work on my own faith. I like to think that the next time I find myself in such a tough situation I will not be so stubborn, and it will be easier for me to exercise my faith.

Jack and other friends have always told me they would be available if I ever needed a blessing. I appreciated that, and I appreciated the fact that they left it up to me. Saying, "I hope you know I'm available if you ever need a blessing" is different from saying, "I can see you are having a hard time, why don't I come over and give you a blessing?" The role of the priesthood holder is to serve others, to teach, and to help people build their faith. Since the responsibility was still on me to ask, just like the handbook says, then the blessing could be according to my faith. If someone had insisted without me seeking it out, then where would the faith be in that?

One of those friends who had told me I could always call on him for a blessing was Glen. When I asked him to come to our home to give me this blessing, this was the first time we had shared with him what had been going on since we still had not told many people.

I told him there were two main things on my mind that I wanted him to consider in the blessing. I needed comfort heading into tomorrow's visit to the hospital for Grace's surgery, and I needed guidance and strength in order to handle my crazy work schedule on top of extra daddy duties while my wife spent most of the day in bed. Glen blessed me with the things I had requested, along with some other things he felt inspired to say.

He then stood with me while I gave Grace another blessing. As the handbook says, since we had already anointed her with oil weeks before, and since this administration was for the same illness, there was no need to use oil again. I felt like this blessing was connected to the first one—like an appendage. Although we still did not have a diagnosis, I was a little more informed this time.

I felt wonderful during the blessing. I felt like the words I was saying were coming from somewhere greater than myself. As soon as I finished and lifted my hands, Grace spun in her chair and wrapped her arms around me. I did not realize it until she brought it to my attention, but the entire blessing had been given with words like, "When you look back on this time ..." and "Someday you will see why ..."

I had done my best to prepare beforehand, and God blessed me with the ability to say what she needed to feel comfort. I felt close to the Spirit as I said those words, and I knew they were true. I was grateful for that.

sixteen

the answer

My parents arrived at our home early the next morning so my dad could ride with us to the hospital and my mom could stay with the kids. We said a prayer together and then left to make it there by 5:30 a.m. Her operation was not actually scheduled until 7:00 a.m., which would have been a long time to sit around even if it were a normal day. On a day like this, when our emotions were already fragile, the extra time was pure torture.

Nurses popped in and out of the room during that hour and a half, but the doctor did not show up until the scheduled time. After Grace was hooked up to her IV and they were wheeling her out of the room, the doctor turned to me and said there was a possibility he might have an answer within a few hours.

My stomach lurched when he said that. I had been under the impression that it would be days before we would have an answer—after the results came back from the lab. Now that I knew there was a possibility I could know within a few hours, anticipation threatened to pulverize my nerves like last time.

Dad and I gave our contact information to the lady at the front desk, and we left the building. I had purposefully saved some of my work deliveries for that morning so we would have something to do besides sit around the hospital.

I could hardly think straight as Dad and I drove around the valley. I was so glad to have him there with me— much more than I think he knew. Since my mind was fixated on the trial I was going through at the moment, I asked him to share with me some of the most difficult trials he had gone through in his life.

I loved listening to him talk about those times. It was not so much *what* he was saying as *how* he was saying it. He actually seemed to enjoy reminiscing about the time he lost his job forty years earlier, right before my big sister was born. He was not as fond of the memories surrounding the year the Navy kept him away from his family, but I enjoyed the way he was proud of the decisions he made during that time.

It brought peace to my heart to listen to him because it helped me believe someday I might be able to look back on my trials with fondness. It gave me fuel to want to be the best man I could be so I could someday look back and be proud of the decisions I made when times were hardest. And, of course, it was nice to listen to someone else's struggles because it helped me feel like Grace and I were not the only ones in this world with problems.

After being away from the hospital for about an hour and a half, we drove back. This procedure was expected to take longer than the first biopsy, but we didn't know how long that might be. Dad offered to buy me breakfast in the cafeteria, and at first I agreed. I thought it would be wise to try to put something in my belly since I was already feeling weak, but as soon as we stepped into the cafeteria I knew there was no way I could eat anything.

Dad offered me a granola bar from his backpack, which I did my best to eat. I worked on that granola bar the entire time Dad had his meal, but I was only able to consume half of it, and even that much felt like a feast. I wrapped the rest of it up to save in my pocket.

We spent the remaining time in the waiting area of the surgery wing. For the next forty-five minutes I watched the door for the doctor or nurse.

When the doctor did finally walk through that door, my heart jumped. I monitored the expression on his face, trying to read him before he even had a chance to talk, but that was of no use. He did have a bright smile, but he was the type of man who always had one. He had done this surgery hundreds of times, and I doubted he would come in crying if it was bad news.

He sat down on the seat directly in front of me and said, "Well, the samples do still have to go to the lab, and I have to leave the actual diagnosis up to your specialist, but I can tell you I found no cancer."

Wait. What? He said he didn't *find* any cancer, but he didn't say there *was* none. I asked him to clarify.

"It's almost certainly sarcoidosis," he said. "There's a small possibility the lab will say it's something else, but I'm confident it's not cancer." I cried on the inside, but smiled on the outside. I made him tell me two more times to make sure I understood him correctly.

I wanted to run down the hall and find my wife, but that would not be allowed for another hour—not until she was awake. I called and sent text messages to our closest family and friends—those who had been waiting in anticipation along with us.

Some of the returned texts said things like, "God is so good," and "I knew God loved you guys." I didn't say anything in response to those words, but I did take issue with them. I mean, God is good whether my wife had cancer or not. To say He loves us because she was diagnosed with something different than cancer ... would that imply that He somehow does not love people with cancer as much? Nonsense.

I was grateful she would not have to go through chemotherapy. I was grateful the mortality rate from sarcoidosis is small compared to something as serious as lymphoma. That said, I also knew sarcoidosis was an auto-immune disorder and we were just starting down what was going to be a very long road. There is no cure for sarcoidosis. There are only ways to treat the symptoms and hope the body can figure out how to fix itself. Some people get better. Some people never do. But from what all of the doctors had been telling us, this was definitely the more favorable diagnosis.

An hour passed before I was allowed to go see my beautiful Grace. I walked into the room with an enormous smile of relief on my face. When she saw me, she immediately started to cry. She had only been partly coherent when the doctor talked to her, and she was not sure if she was remembering his words correctly. When I came in and she saw my expression, she knew it was good news without having to say a word.

"I get to watch my babies grow up," she said.

seventeen

God's hand in our life

Recovery from this surgery was much harder than after the previous biopsy. For three and a half days the farthest she went from the bed was just to the bathroom, and even that journey made her feel like she was going to pass out. My mother stayed with us for five days to watch the kids and help around the house while I was at work. She finally went home after I got off work on Friday.

On that day, before I had gone to work, I got up early and shoveled three inches of snow off the sidewalk and driveway. It was the first snowfall of the season, and I wanted to have the walks clear so I would not have to do it after work. I knew I would not be able to put off that chore until the next day because I was going to have to be somewhere early Saturday morning. I had already learned from past experience that waiting too long to shovel the driveway meant that it could turn to solid ice and become a problem.

I woke up early that Friday morning to shovel that snow because I ached to spend time with my children. I wanted to come home from work and take them out on the sled while it was still light. My mother had done a great job playing the role of Grandma all week, but the kids were feeling the effects of being out of their normal routine, and I wanted to give them some Daddy time.

All day at work, though, I watched through the window as the snow continued to fall. We received another eight inches by the time I got home. My attempt to clear the driveway and walks before work was all for nothing.

I went through the closets to dig out my snow clothes, all the while debating within myself whether I was going to spend the last hour of sunlight with a shovel in my hand, or pulling two kids on the sled. I went back and forth with my decision. One minute I would convince myself it would not be so bad to let the snow sit for a few more days, even though I had done that in the past and got the car stuck in the driveway. The next minute I would decide otherwise.

I started leaning toward the idea of taking the kids out on the sled, and then I would shovel snow late at night in the dark after Grace and the kids were asleep. As I was pulling on my boots, I watched through the window as a pickup truck pulled up to the house. I recognized the two men who jumped out, so I quickly ran out to join them. They not only brought snow shovels, but they also brought their gas powered snow blower.

I knew they had no idea I had been debating all afternoon whether or not to shovel snow or go play with my children. I immediately remembered the blessing Glen had given me five days earlier that promised I would be able to keep up with both work and my fatherly duties. I knew these two men had no idea just how much it meant to me that they would show up so unexpectedly to serve us.

The three of us had the driveway and sidewalks cleared in a fraction of the time it would have taken me to do it on my own, leaving me with enough time to bundle my kids up for a ride on the sled. I pulled them all around the neighborhood until the sun was down and my back hurt.

That little miracle might not seem like much to someone else, but it meant everything to me. The entire time I trudged through the snow with my kids, I could not help but smile. That blessing was so specific to my needs, and so specific to what Glen had blessed me with, that nobody will ever convince me it was coincidence. Those two men had never showed up to shovel my walk before, and I know nobody called or asked them to come do it. They just felt impressed to come. I knew it was God's way of showing His hand in my life. I will always have that special little piece of His love as part of my testimony of Him.

* * *

The lab results soon came back and Grace's specialist confirmed what the surgeon had said. It was sarcoidosis—one of the most serious cases he had ever seen. He immediately started her on a treatment plan, which included a whole fistful of pills with terrible side effects. She was far from cured, but she immediately started to feel good enough to be out of bed. It would be a long time before she would be up to full speed again, but at least she could keep up with most of her daily routine.

A while later, when I looked back at the records I keep for work, I noticed a big dip in my work load, followed by a big increase. During the weeks when our trial was most difficult, I had only about half as much work as normal come in. It felt like a lot more since I was only working at half my usual speed. My smaller workload made it possible to take time off to accompany Grace to her appointments and hospital procedures.

Immediately after Grace started feeling better, my workload doubled. I had to work some late nights over the next month, but Grace now had the stamina to keep up with the kids and whatever else she needed to do. Most importantly, especially with the hospital bills piling up, the sudden increase in workload brought our income back to normal. That was a miracle. The dip in my workload had made it possible to keep up when times were toughest, and then the big bump in workload made it so we were not as far behind financially as we might have been. It was the best of both worlds.

eighteen

grateful for trials?

Our trial with Grace's health is not over yet. She still has a long road ahead of her, but I wholeheartedly believe this illness is not going to ruin or run her life. I have been madly in love with Grace since we first met back in Provo, and this experience made me appreciate her even more.

This brings me to something that had bothered me for years. All my life I have heard people say we should be grateful for our trials. As soon as we can learn to be grateful for our trials, our trials get easier. As soon as we can bend our will to God and be grateful for our trials, we will be much happier, etc.

It is easy for me to say I'm grateful for my time with Amber. Even though our time together ended in heartache, I'm grateful for who she is as a person and for the role she played in my life. I'm grateful for the fact that our experience taught me how to care about people even while they were hurting me. I'm grateful for the lesson I learned in how to lean on my brother, Jesus Christ, when times are tough. I'm grateful for the way that period of my life has helped shape me into who I am now. I'm grateful for the miracles I experienced and the love people showed me while I was feeling so low.

It is easy for me to say those things now because it has been fourteen years since my divorce was finalized. When I was lying in bed late at night, sobbing into my pillow because she left me, it never crossed my mind to get down on my knees and say, "Dear Father in Heaven, I'm so grateful she walked out on me." When I was suffering alone in Grace's hospital room, waiting for her to return from a biopsy, I had no desire to tell God, "I'm so glad my wife might die."

Even if I were to have said those things, God knows my heart. He would have known I did not truly feel that way. Was I an ungrateful son because I was not happy about it in the moment? Was I rejecting God and the Plan of Salvation by being so upset and unwilling to say "thank you" for my pain?

For years I felt like this was what people meant when they said we should be grateful for our trials—that I was an ungrateful person until I could get to the point when I could be glad for them. But there are some trials where I just don't see that being a possibility. If one of my children were to unexpectedly die tomorrow, I can pretty much guarantee I would never be glad it happened.

While Grace and I were still in the hardest part of our big trial, this became the topic of an Elder's Quorum lesson. I felt hypersensitive to people's words as they shared the same basic answers I had heard all my life—the kind that made me feel like an ungrateful son of my Heavenly Father. But then one man raised his hand and said something profound that completely changed my whole outlook.

He said there are different kinds of gratitude. There was, of course, the kind I had been thinking of, but there was also the kind where our actions do the talking. So, what was it God actually wanted us to *do*? The answer was something I had heard a million times before—something God always wants from us. He wants us to have a broken heart and a contrite spirit. In other words, when I find myself in the middle of a trial, the best way to show gratitude would be to humble myself, be submissive, and lean on God like a little child seeking guidance and comfort from parents.

The opposite of that would be to get angry with God. If I were to shake my fist and say, "This just goes to prove God doesn't love me," then I would be missing out on a great opportunity to identify miracles in my life. If I were to choose to numb my mind with alcohol, or pacify myself by taking my credit card on a shopping spree, then I would be putting up a barrier between myself and God when I most needed His presence.

Being humble is an action that shows gratitude. That made perfect sense because I could see how my life had grown closer to Christ every time I was willing to have a broken heart and contrite spirit—to show I could actually consider myself a good son of my Heavenly Father, even while in the midst of a trial, by humbling myself like a little child.

nineteen

even as I am

In a talk given by Elder Dallin H. Oaks during the 2010 Priesthood Session of General Conference, he said, "On some choice occasions I have experienced that certainty of inspiration in a healing blessing and have known that what I was saying was the will of the Lord. However, like most who officiate in healing blessings, I have often struggled with uncertainty on the words I should say. For a variety of causes, every elder experiences increases and decreases in his level of sensitivity to the promptings of the Spirit. Every elder who gives a blessing is subject to influence by what he desires for the person afflicted. Each of these and other mortal imperfections can influence the words we speak.

"Fortunately, the words spoken in a healing blessing are not essential to its healing effect. If faith is sufficient and if the Lord wills it, the afflicted person will be healed or blessed whether the officiator speaks those words or not."

I read this talk at least half a dozen times while Grace and I were going through the toughest parts of our journey. His words gave me a lot of peace, but also raised some questions in my mind. I felt peace upon knowing that my wife's healing was not dependent upon whether or not I said those specific words in her blessing. At the same time, I wondered whether or not my words mattered at all. If God is going to do His thing, whether I say it or not, do any of my words matter? If I'm giving a blessing, wouldn't it be best if I just said, "I bless you with all of the things God has in store for you," and then leave it at that? After all, the blessings are predicated upon the faith of the receiver, not on the words of the giver, right?

I studied, prayed, and pondered on the matter, but it took me quite a while to find an answer that felt right. Although I spent a lot of time searching and praying for the answer, it did not come while I was on my knees or while I had my nose in a book. It came to me while I was simply going about my daily business. I did not hear the words audibly, but they came to my mind very clearly, and the more I thought about them, the broader my understanding became.

I thought of the scripture in 3 Nephi 27:27 when Christ came to the American continent and was talking to the Nephites. He said, "... Therefore, what manner of men ought ye to be? Verily I say unto you, even as I am."

I had heard that scripture hundreds of times throughout my life, but it had never hit me this deeply before. As I thought about it, my mind focused on two different meanings.

The first meaning was in regards to Christ's actions. He had just died on the cross and was appearing for the first time to the Nephites with his resurrected body. And what were the first things He did when He appeared to them? He let them feel the wounds in His hands, feet, and side so the people might know Him. He administered the sacrament. He taught them. And, yes, He healed people of all kinds of infirmities, and He laid His hands on them to bless them.

Holding the priesthood means I am called by God to act in Jesus Christ's name. I am called to do what I think Jesus would do if He were here. When Jesus was with the people, He did not tell them to go pray and ask to be made whole. He told them to have faith, and He blessed them to be whole. There is a difference.

In the same talk, Elder Oaks went on to say, "Conversely, if the officiator yields to personal desire or inexperience and gives commands or words of blessing in excess of what the Lord chooses to bestow according to the faith of the individual, those words will not be fulfilled."

That's the hard part, isn't it? I continued to think that if my duty is to act as Christ would act, and not to yield to my own desires, then how could I possibly differentiate between what Christ wants and what I want or incorrectly *think* Christ wants?

For me, the answer lies in the same scripture I quoted before. What manner of a man am I supposed to be? I am supposed to be like Christ. I need to live my life like Christ in all aspects—in everything I do. If I strive every day to be like Him—learning as much about Him as I can, and putting that knowledge into practice—then I will grow to be more and more like Him. The more I am like Him on a day-to-day basis, the easier it will be for me to act as He would act. If I am like Him, I could more easily perform a blessing in His name, understanding and knowing what His will might be because my will would mirror His. If I go throughout my days making no effort to *know* Christ, and the only time I try to align my heart with His is while I'm trying to give a blessing, then I will be at a loss for words every time.

I do not expect to master this ability in this life. Even if I live to be a hundred, I expect to still be striving to know Christ in order to be like Him.

When someone knows Christ, it shines in their countenance. I'm not one of those church members who's lucky enough to be around general authorities on regular occasions, but I did attend a temple wedding once where Elder Neil A. Maxwell, who was an apostle at the time, performed the sealing. He spoke about Christ for a short time before performing the sealing. He did not say anything I hadn't really heard before, but the way he said it left a profound impression on me. There was something in his tone that left no doubt he knew Christ. He spoke about Jesus with a level of familiarity as if Jesus lived next door.

As a priesthood holder, that is my goal. I want to get to know Christ so well that my will might mirror His, and I can become better and better at acting in His name. When I do that, that familiarity can radiate from me, and the person receiving the blessing will be able to feel that. If someone can feel Christ's light radiating from me because I know Him, then I can more effectively help that person build their own faith. And their faith is at the center of the blessing they receive.

If I were to only bless someone with "whatever God has in store for you," then I'm putting the responsibility back on God. It would be like saying, "I'm too afraid of saying the wrong thing, so I'm not going to try." The opposite of faith is fear, and that would radiate from me just as much as Christ's light would, which would have the opposite effect on those to whom I'm administering.

The second deep impression that scripture in 3 Nephi left on my mind was about my destiny beyond this life. The LDS church that, as children of God, we all have divine potential. I believe that I am here on earth to gain experience, learn, and progress. I will not be perfect when I die, but through the atonement of Jesus Christ, and through more learning and progression after this life, there are no limits on my ability to progress. In essence, when Jesus said those words, "... what manner of men ought ye to be? Verily I say unto you, even as I am," I believe Christ was talking literally. We are to strive to be like Him in this life, and we are to continue to strive to be like Him as we progress after this life. I want to be like Jesus, but I have a lot yet to learn and a long way to go.

I am good at a number of things. I am good at my job. I am an accomplished singer and musician. I was one of the better pitchers on my high school varsity baseball team. How did I learn to do any of those things?

Practice.

When I formed my first band as a teenager, I had the hardest time singing in tune. I was twenty-two when I recorded my first album, and I had to record the same vocal tracks multiple times in hopes that I might get lucky and have one take that did not have me singing flat. Not only did I lack the skill to produce a quality pitch and tone with my voice, but I lacked the ability to even hear the difference. The other members of my band and the audio engineer repeatedly told me I was singing flat, but I just could not hear the difference.

I took voice lessons. I practiced every day. I sang in the car. I even had a coworker tell me once that she always knew when I arrived at the office because I was always singing when I came through the door. Over the years, I have gained a greater ability to sing in tune and have become very good at hearing the difference. I'm very confident with my voice now, and that did not come by chance.

I see the concept of giving priesthood blessings just the same as singing. Being able to act in the name of Christ takes practice. Like singing everywhere I go, I need to keep a prayer in my heart at all times and always strive to act according to how I think Christ would act—not just while I'm giving a blessing. Like taking singing lessons, I need to put forth an effort to get as much out of my church meetings as I can and always strive for deeper learning through personal study.

Just like how I used to sing flat and could not hear the difference, I cannot expect to be able to "hear" the promptings of the Spirit if I have not worked hard to train my spiritual ear. As a holder of the Melchizedek priesthood, I have the opportunity to act in Christ's name. As was the case with the blessings I mentioned earlier in this book, I still struggle at times to know whether or not I am in tune. Sometimes I'm dead on, and sometimes I'm a little flat. Christ knows me, and He knows I am not going to be perfectly in tune every time. He is gracious enough to let me keep working at it. I am practicing. I am giving it my all, and that's what He asks of me.

If I were to say, "Since it does not matter what I say, then I'll just bless people to receive whatever blessing God has in store for them," that would not be taking my priesthood responsibilities seriously.

Again, I expect to have to work on this all my life, even if I live to be a hundred years old. Much like learning to sing, simply having a strong desire is not enough. It takes work to learn to be in tune, and it takes effort to know the difference.

Understanding this concept has affected all aspects of my spiritual life. I have been called to serve in a wide variety of positions, from choir director to Elders' Quorum President. No matter what I am called to do in the church or in my personal life, the same principle applies. I must train my spiritual ear in a way that I can hear and recognize the Spirit and know when my decisions and actions are in tune.

I must try my very best to know Christ and to act as I think He would act. A big part of the Plan of Salvation is to gain experience, and a big part of gaining experience is learning from our mistakes. It would have been impossible for me to learn to sing only from books, or even just by observing others. I am grateful for the chance to practice being like Christ, even though Christ knows my shortcomings. I pray that I can always grow closer to knowing Him so that others might feel Him near when I act in His name.

Russell would love to hear from you. He reads every review left for his books on Amazon, iTunes, Goodreads, and all the other platforms. Also, if you'd like to join his email list (don't worry, he won't overload your box. He'll just let you know when something new is out), or if you'd just like to write him an email, he would love for you to write him at:

RUSSMCCONKIE@GMAIL.COM

Don't miss these other books by
B. Russell McConkie:

Genesis Evolution:
A Unique Way of Uniting Christianity and Science
Science and religion are not at odds with each other. Told in "everyday language" so you don't have to be a physicist to understand, Genesis Evolution explains the geological history of our earth and places it side-by-side with the entire first chapter of Genesis. It's remarkable how closely the two lock together! It will really make you think... if you let it.

Mormon Missionary Poetry:
A Witty Poem Every Week of a Two Year LDS Mission
The lighter side of the LDS mission life, Mormon Missionary Poetry will make you chuckle with every rhyme and punchline. Starting while he was still in the Missionary Training Center (MTC) and continuing during his two-year mission in Guatemala, Elder Russell McConkie wrote one clever poem every week to send hom to his family.

50370374R00058

Made in the USA
Charleston, SC
22 December 2015